Man

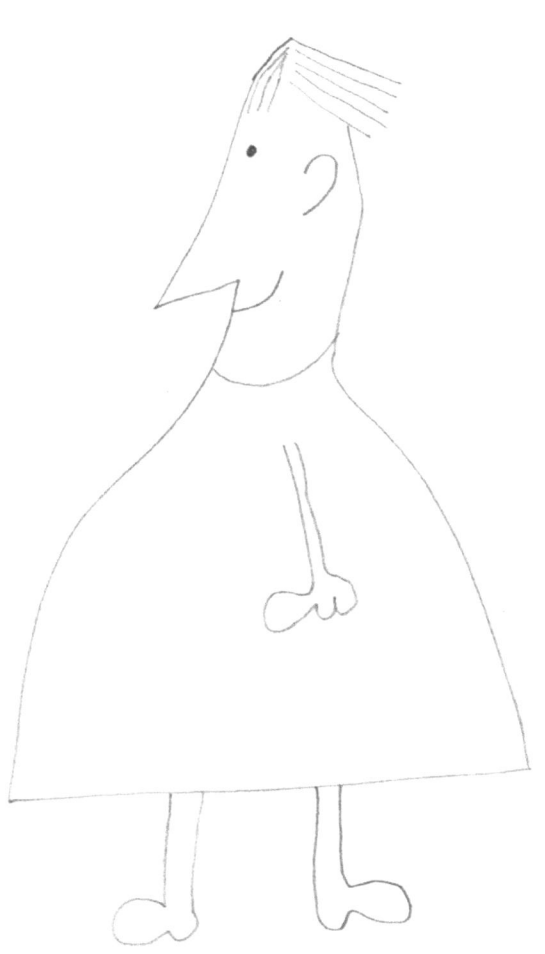

# Woman

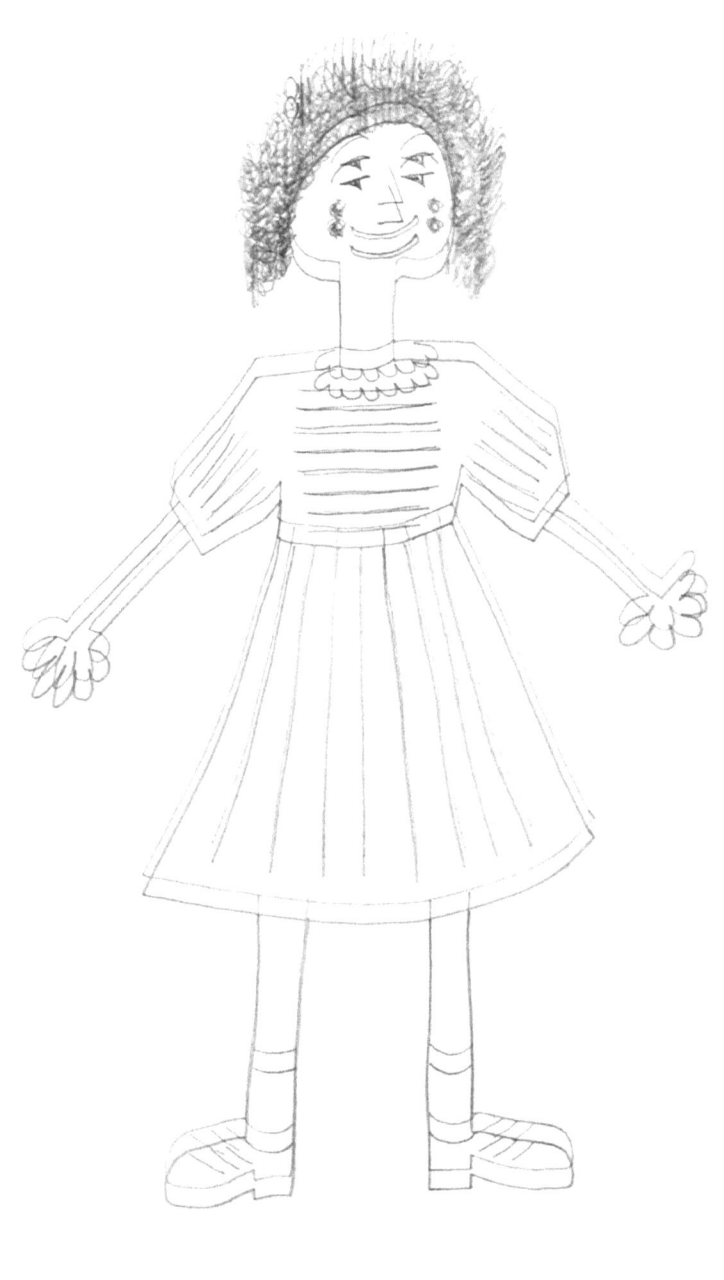

# Loops
# Loops

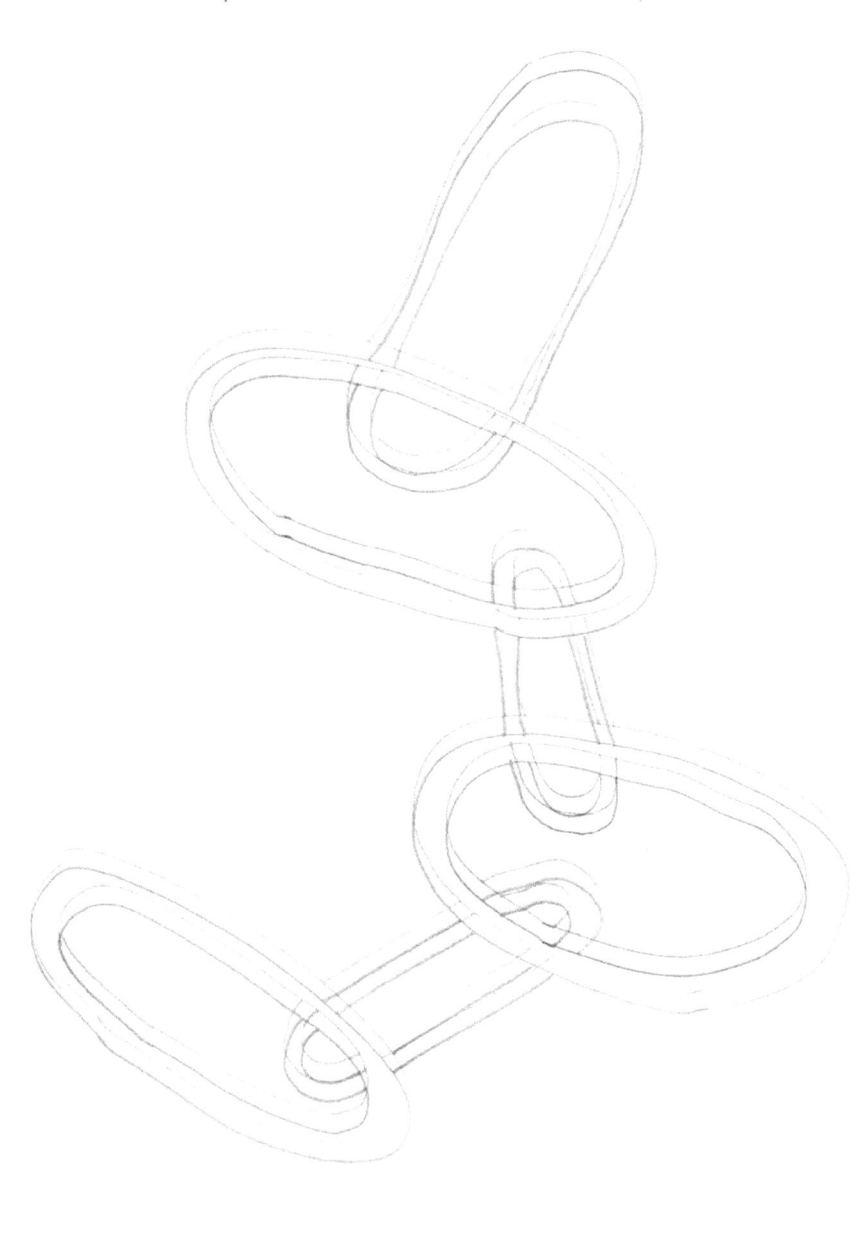

# Bird

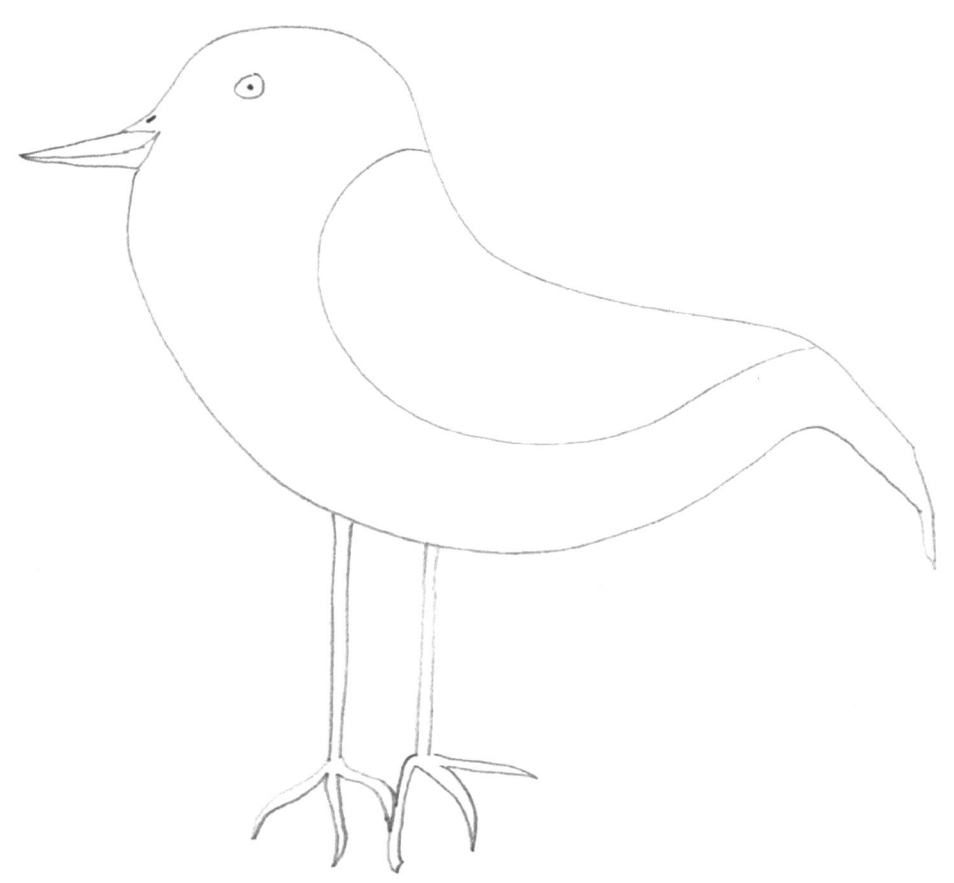

# Butterfly

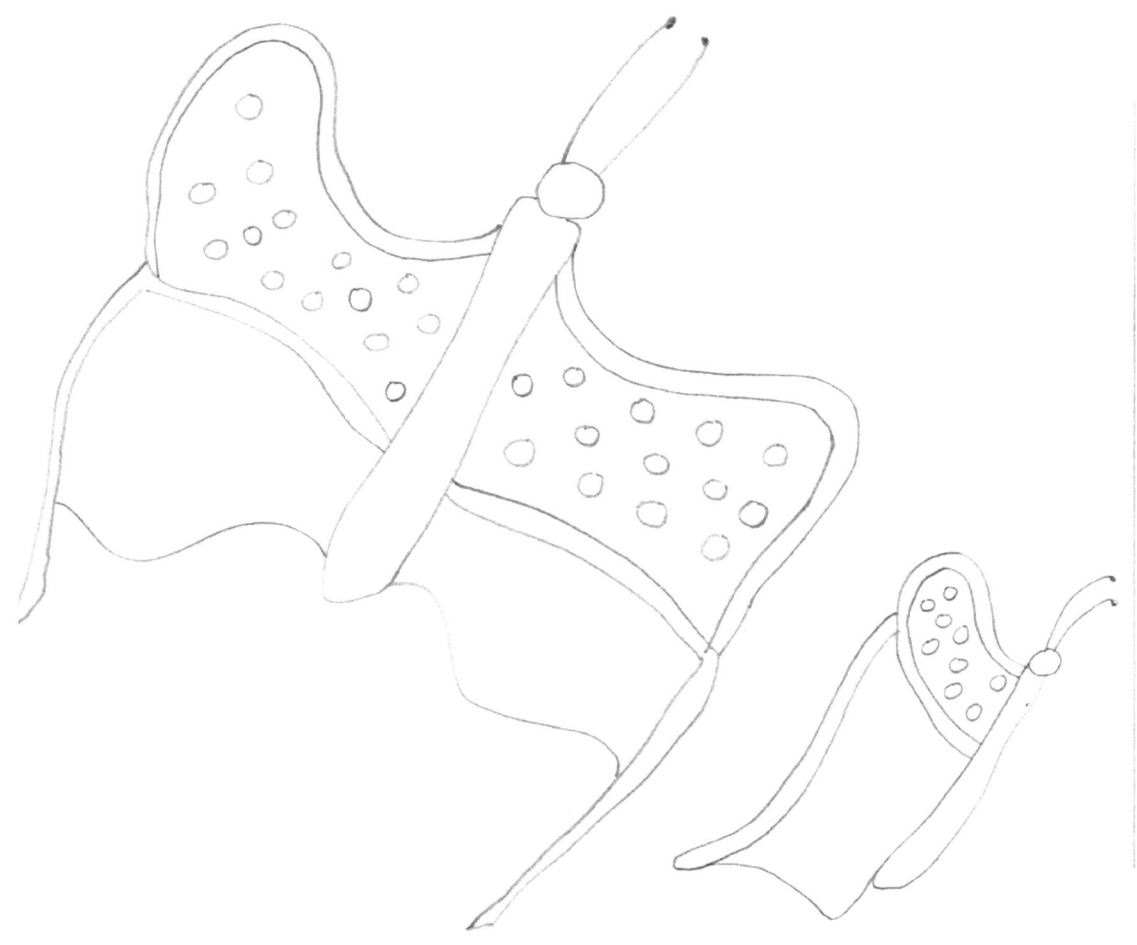

Fish
Fish

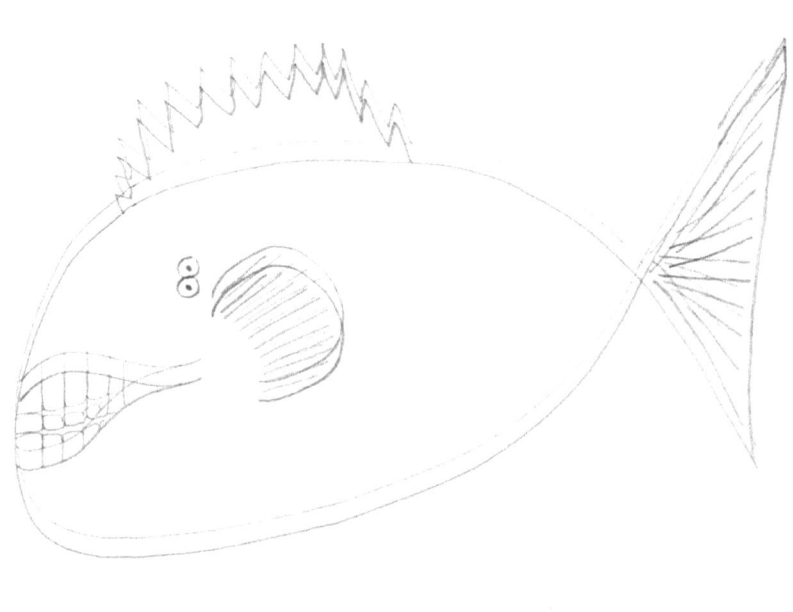

# Clock

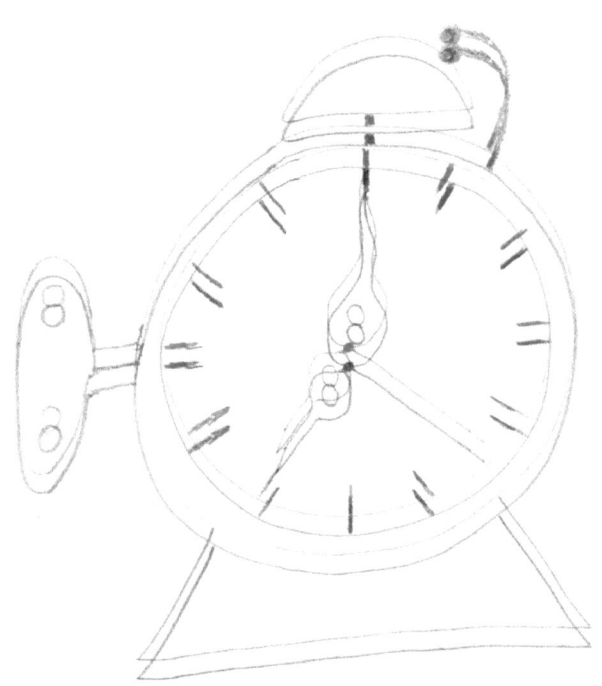

# Robot

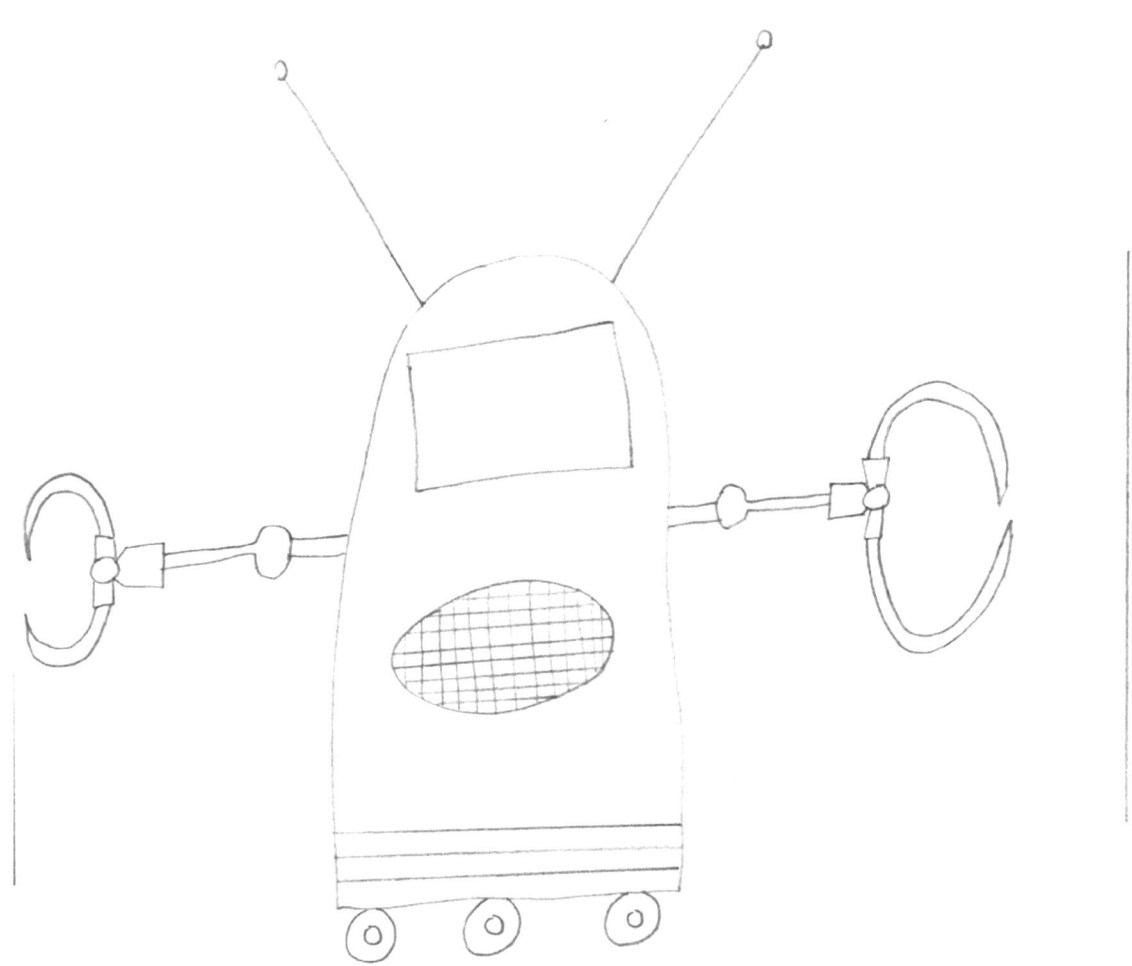

# Book

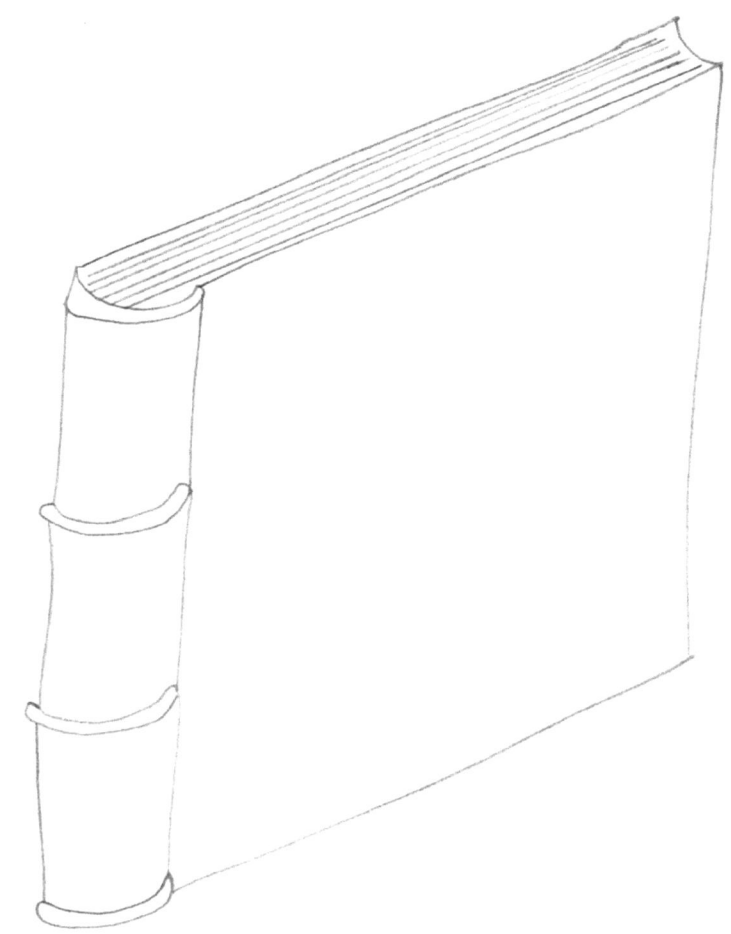

Violin
Violin

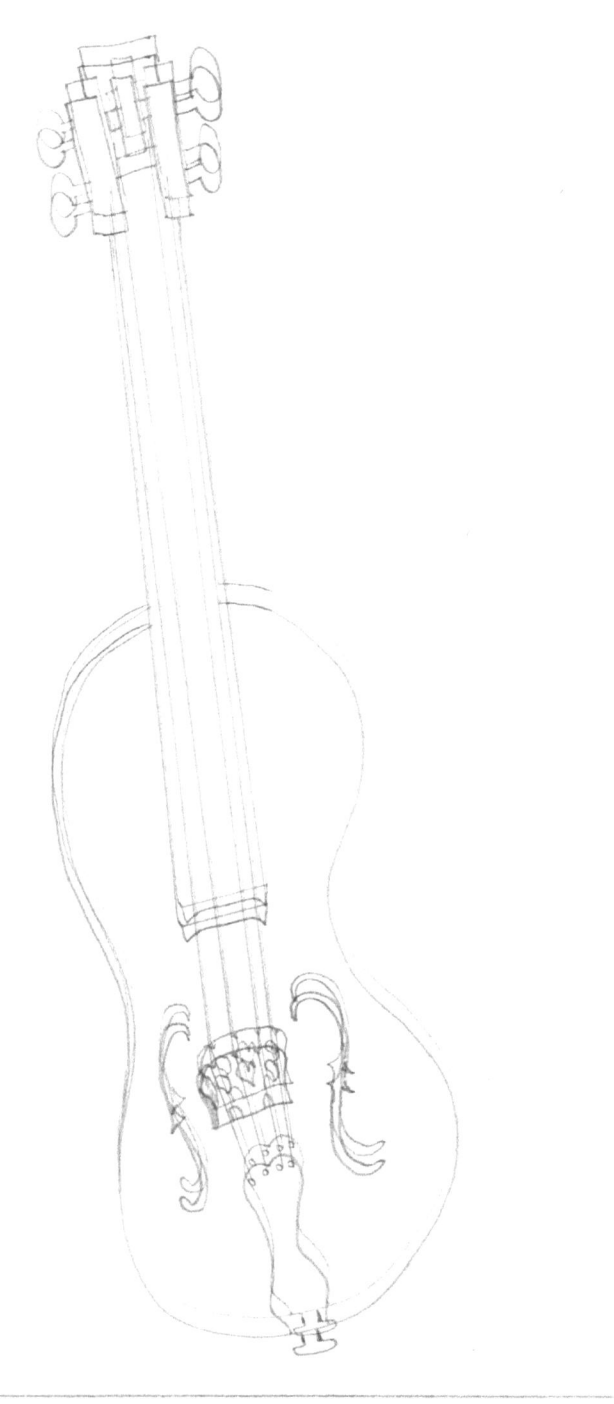

# Machine
# Machine

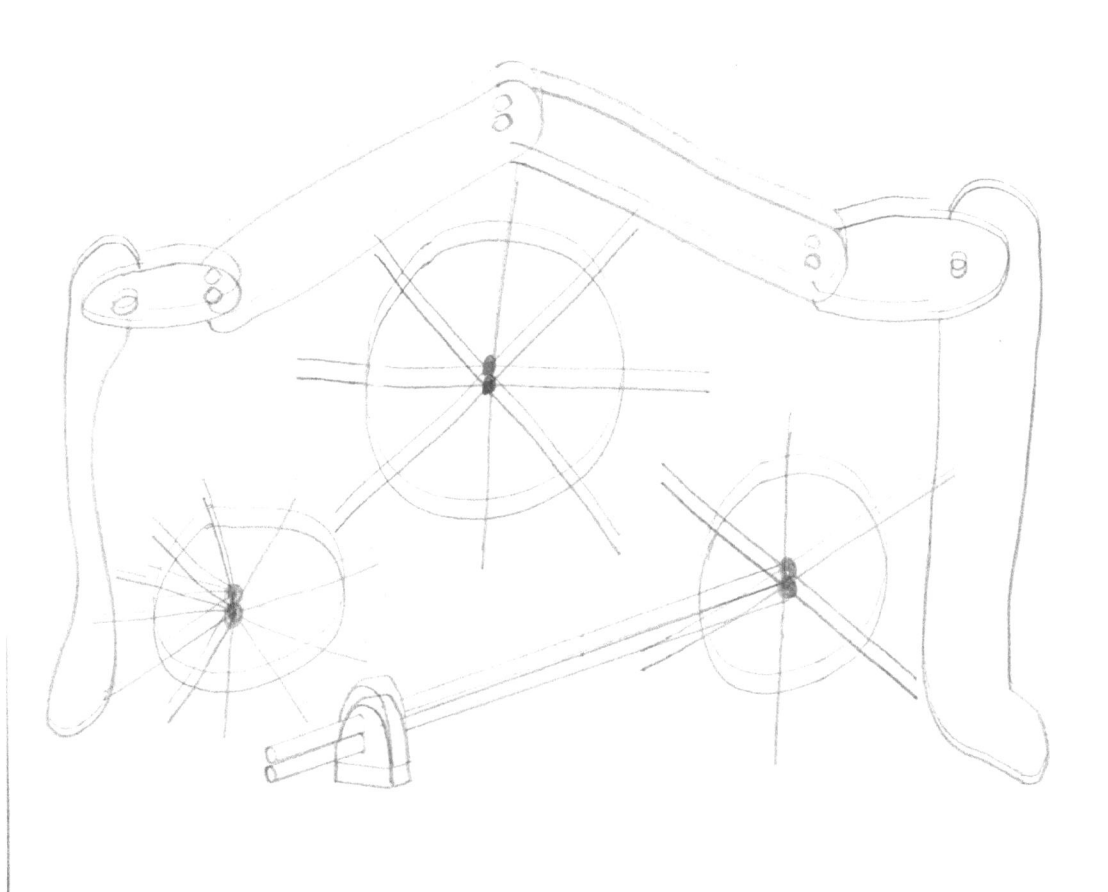

# Star

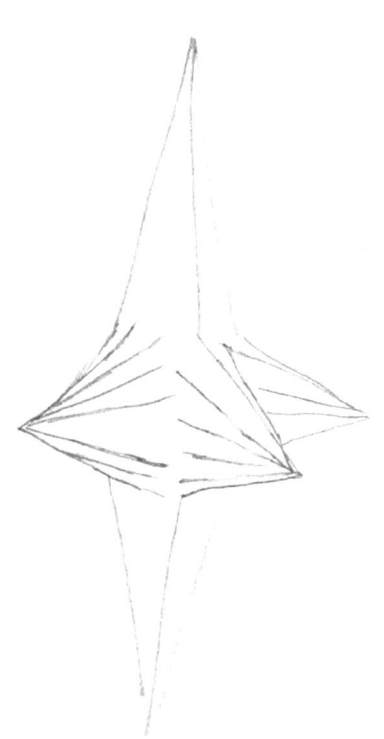

# Shack

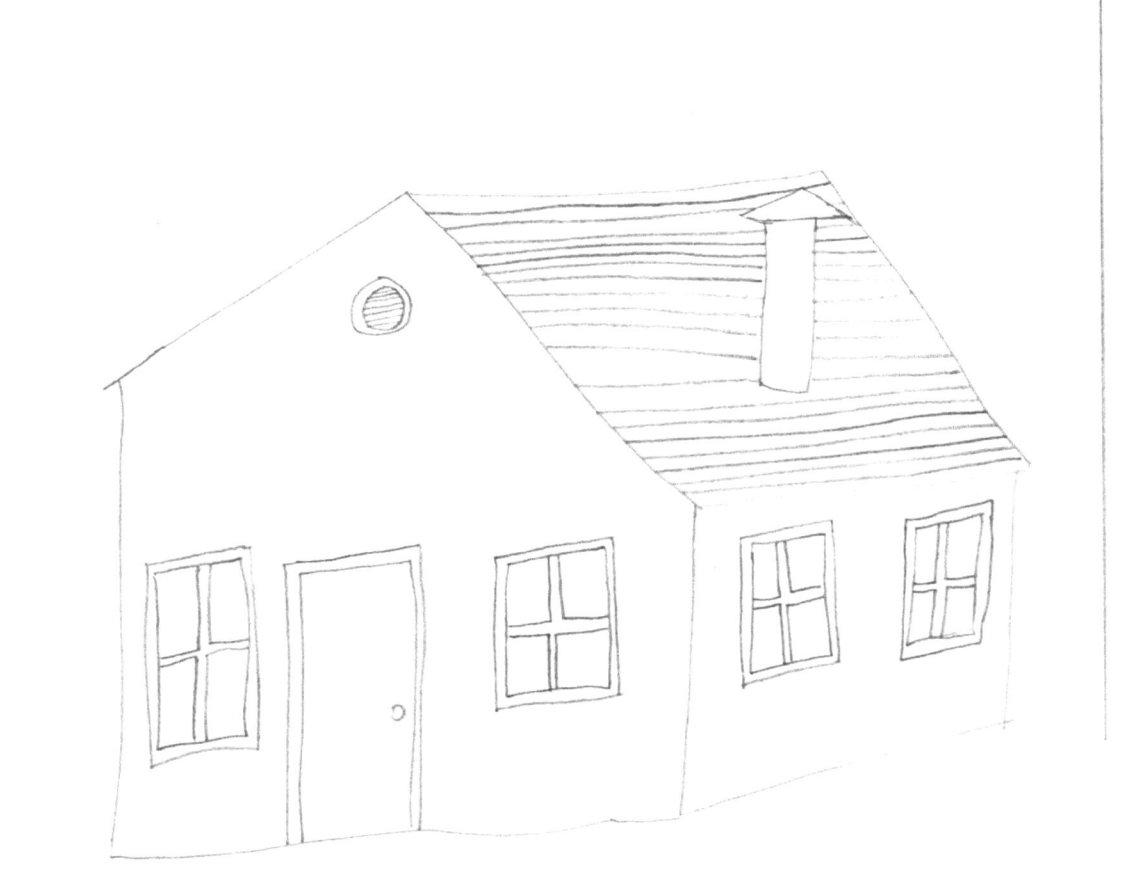

# Railroad Car

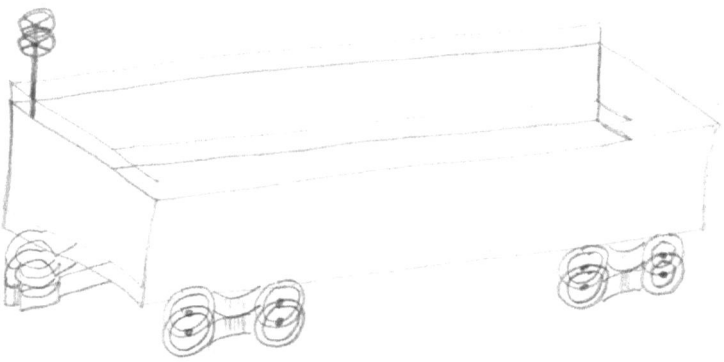

Hope
Hope

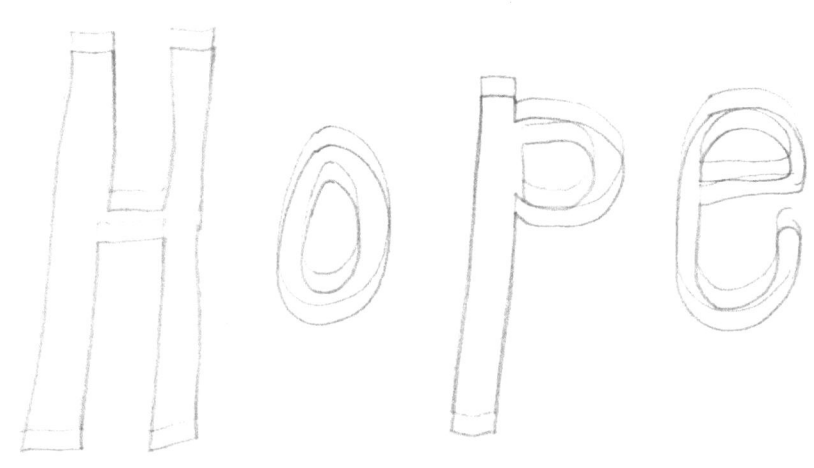

Love

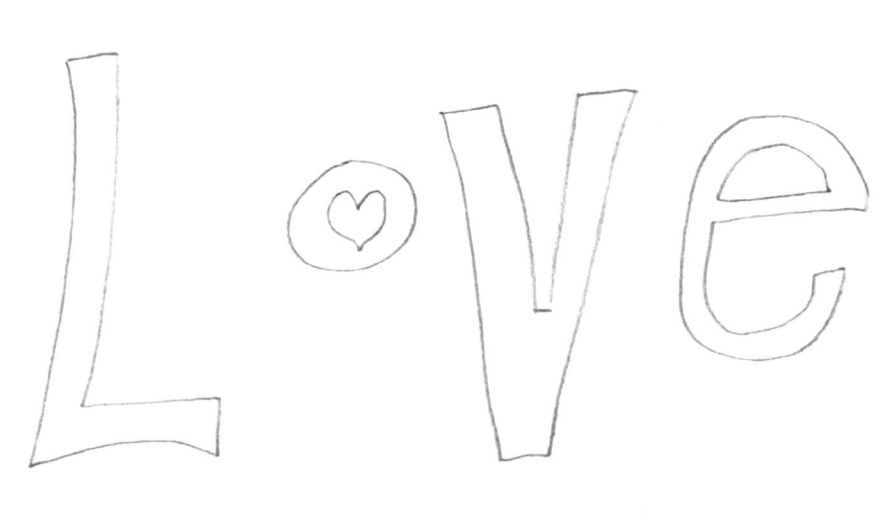

Success

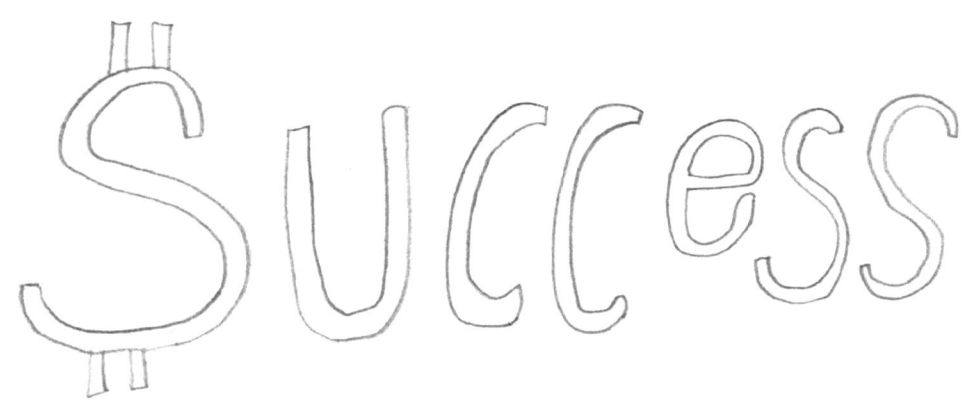

Failure
Failure

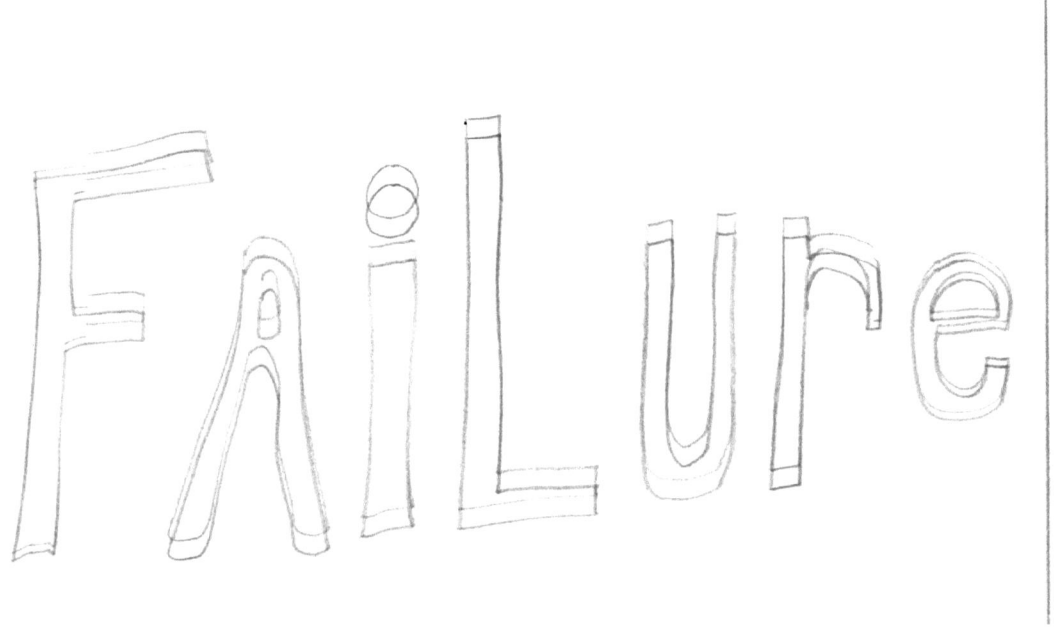

# Faces

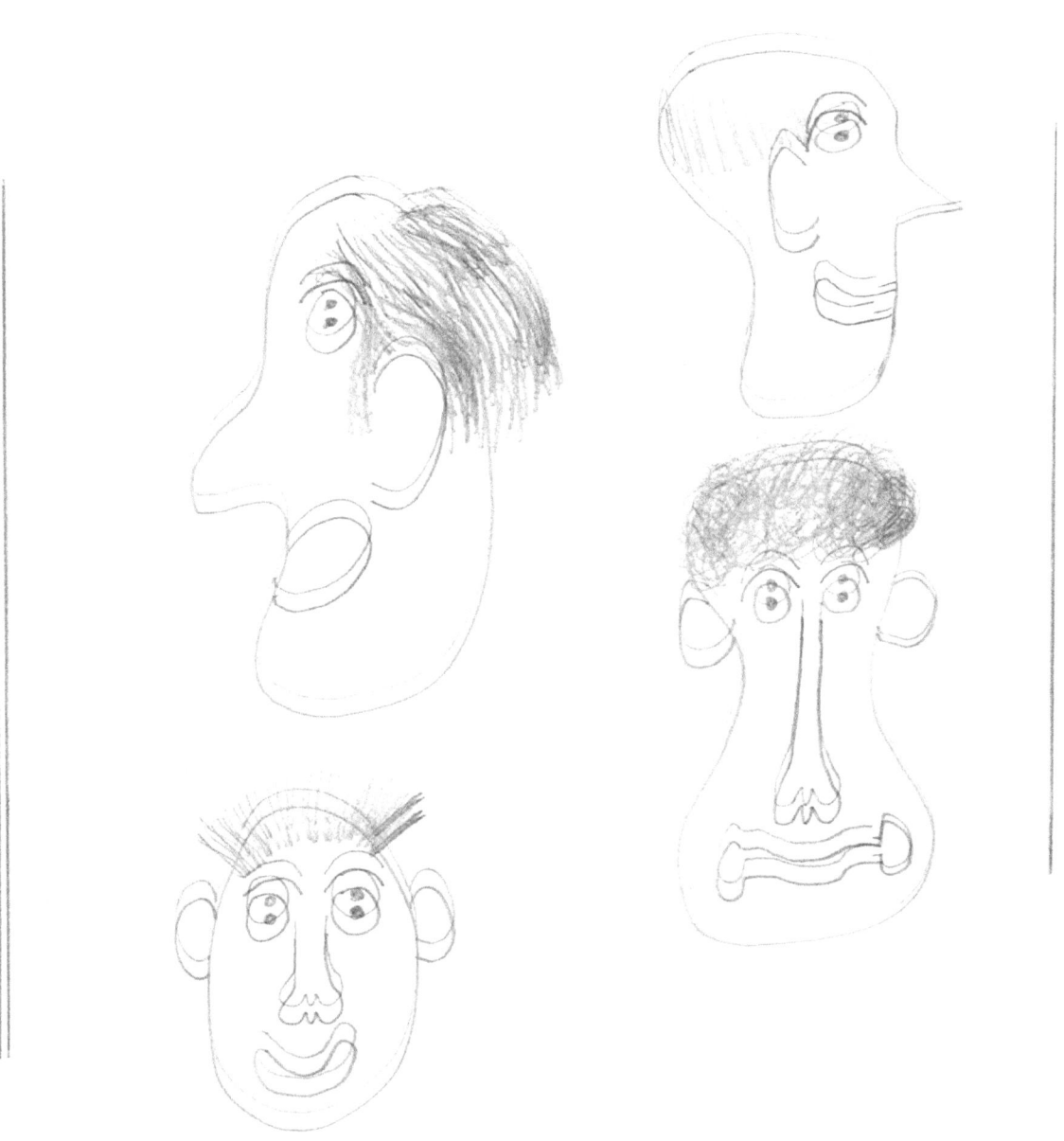

Color Drawings:
These are the Zart people (Art People).
They created the following colorful pictures of the Flower Pots.

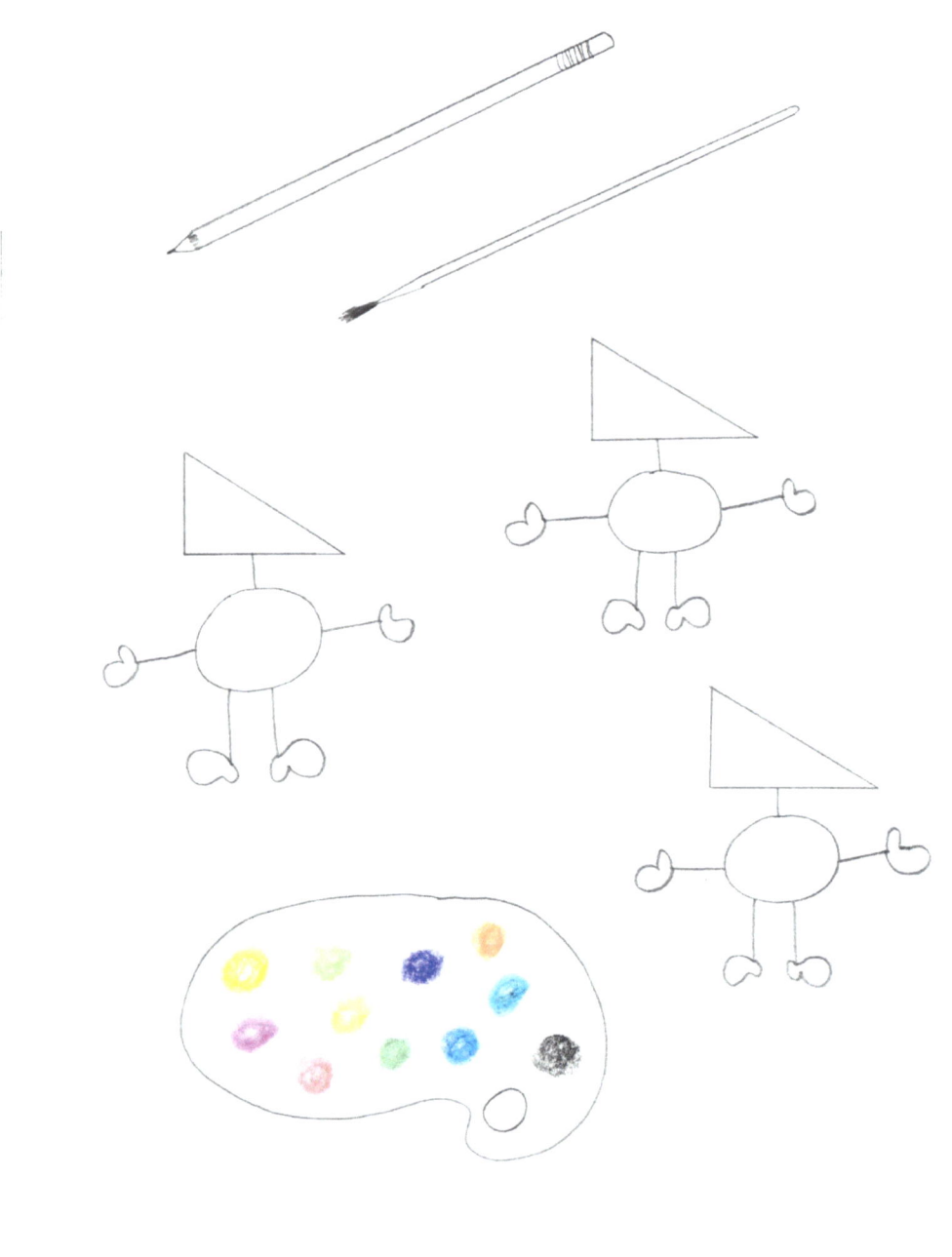

Color Drawing 1

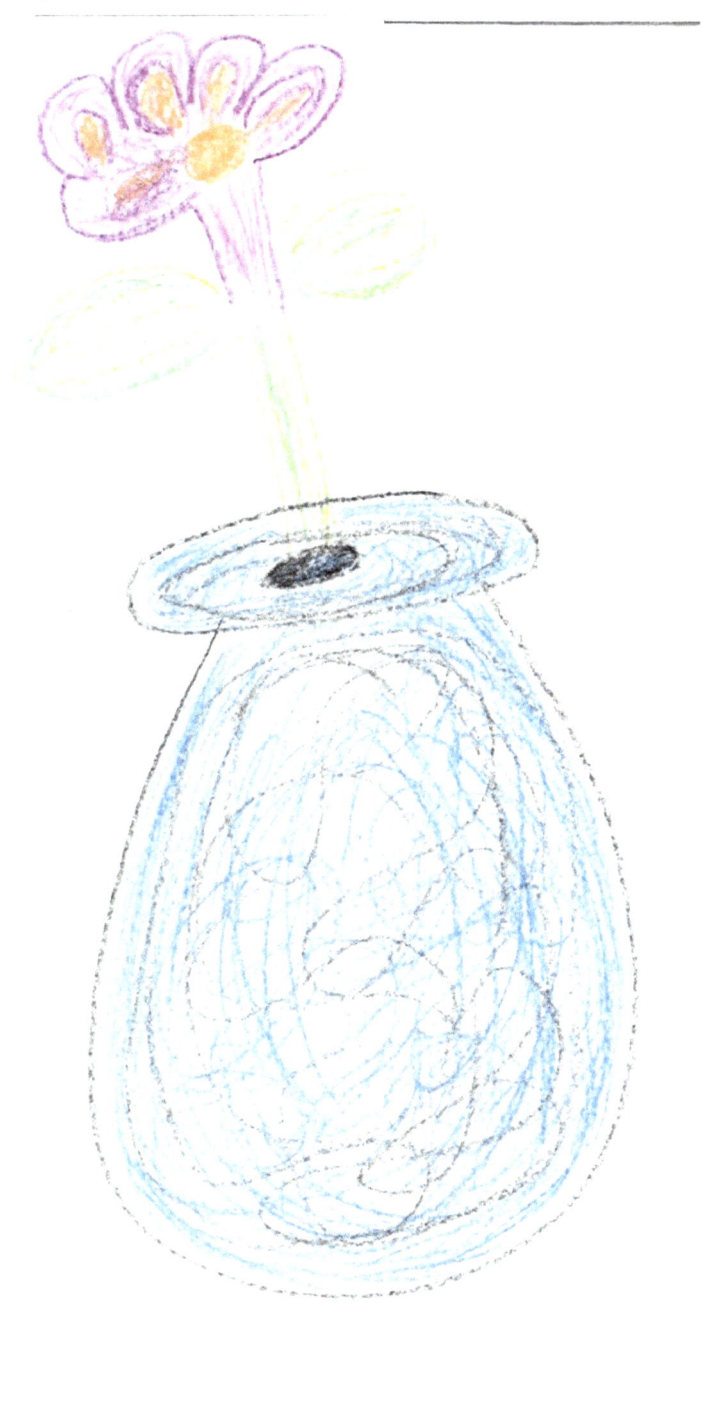

## Color Drawing 2

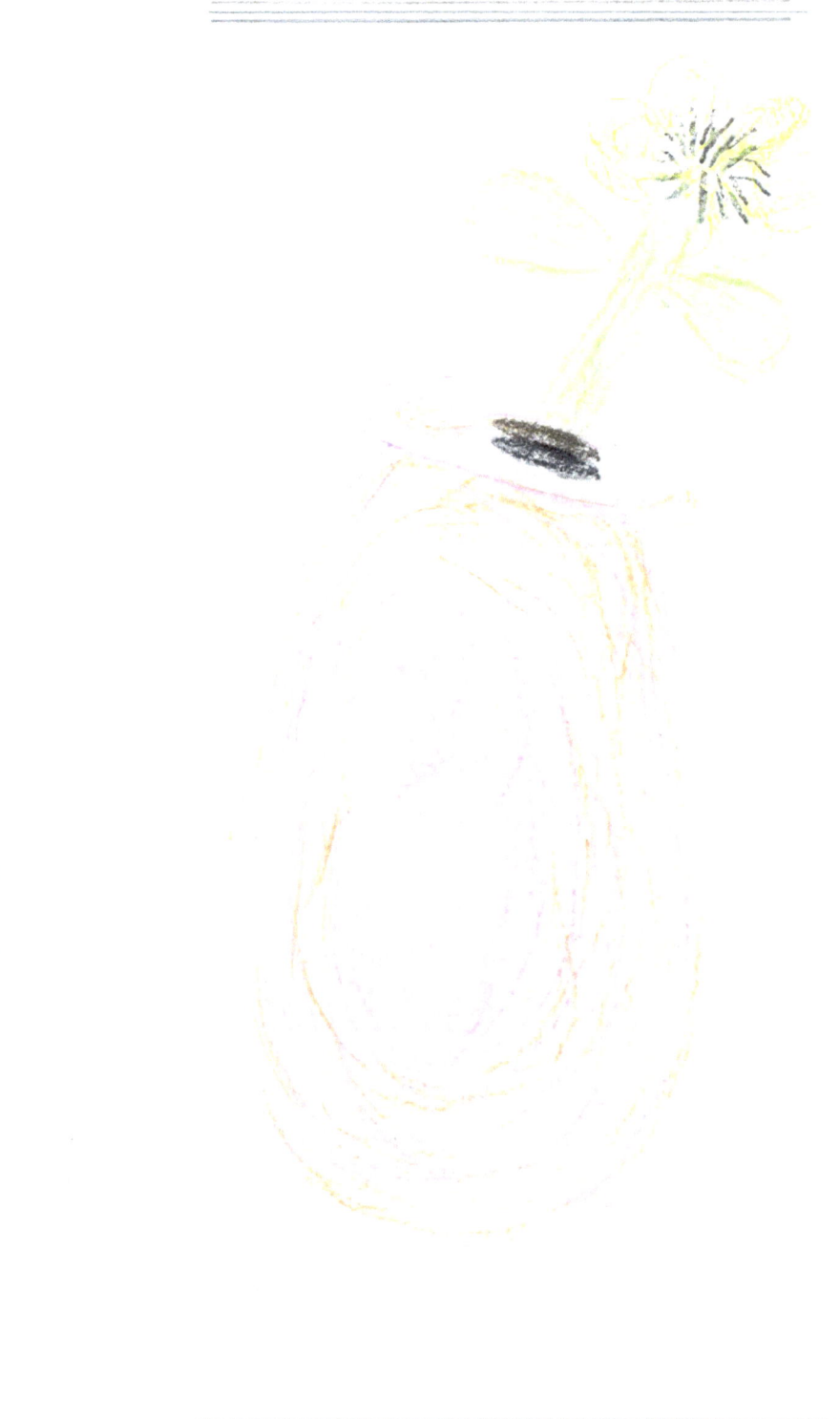

## Color Drawing 3

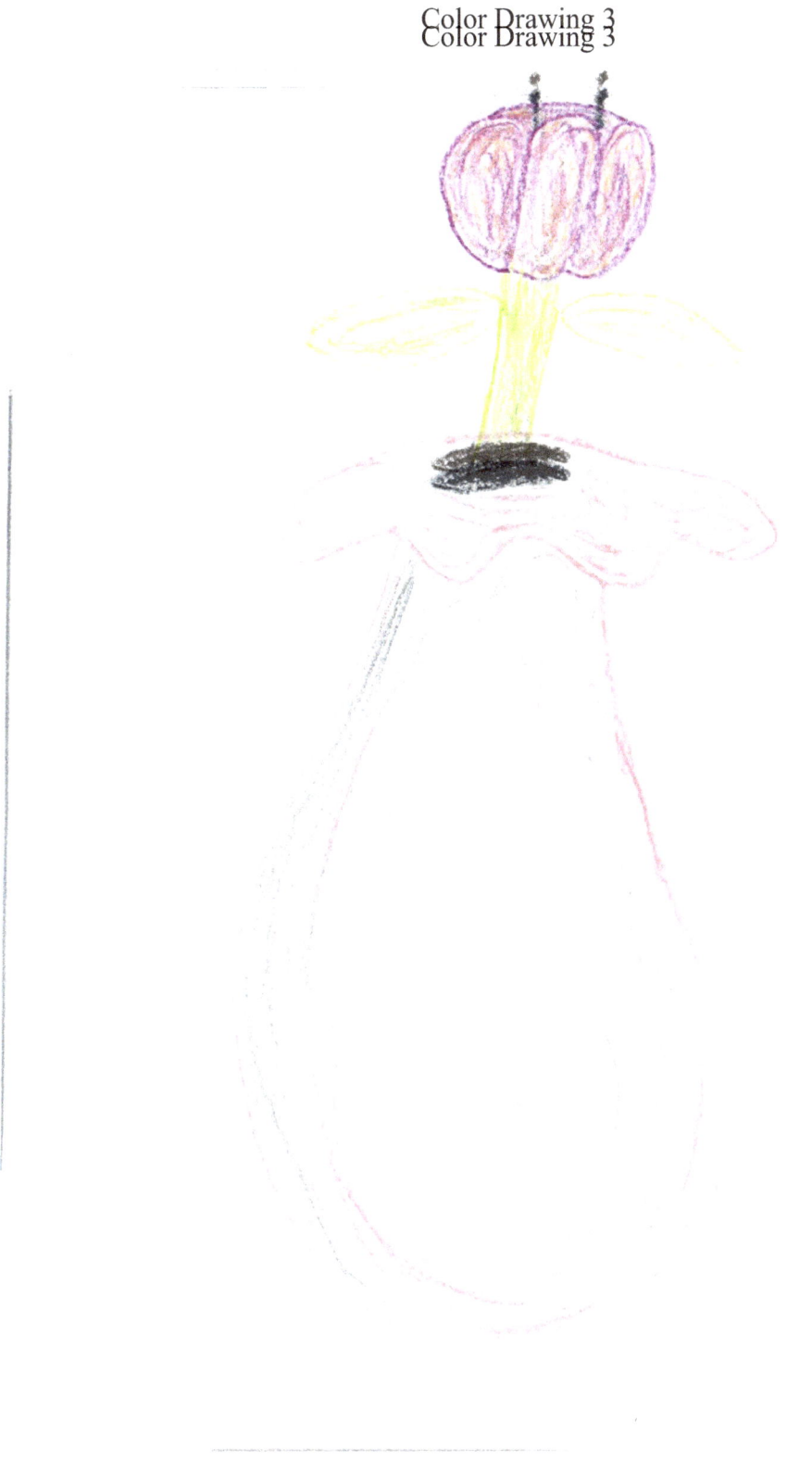

Color Drawing 4

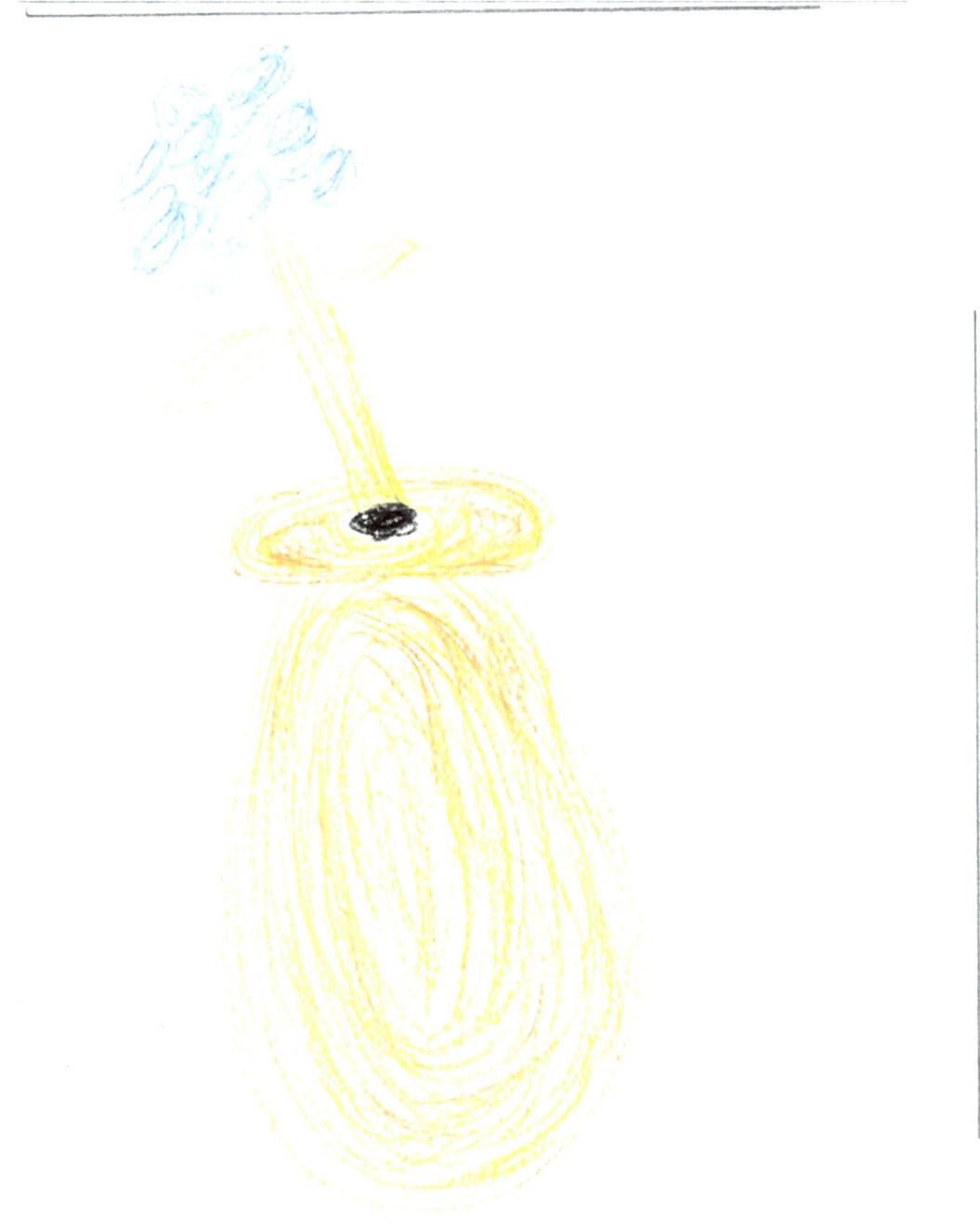

Color Drawing 5

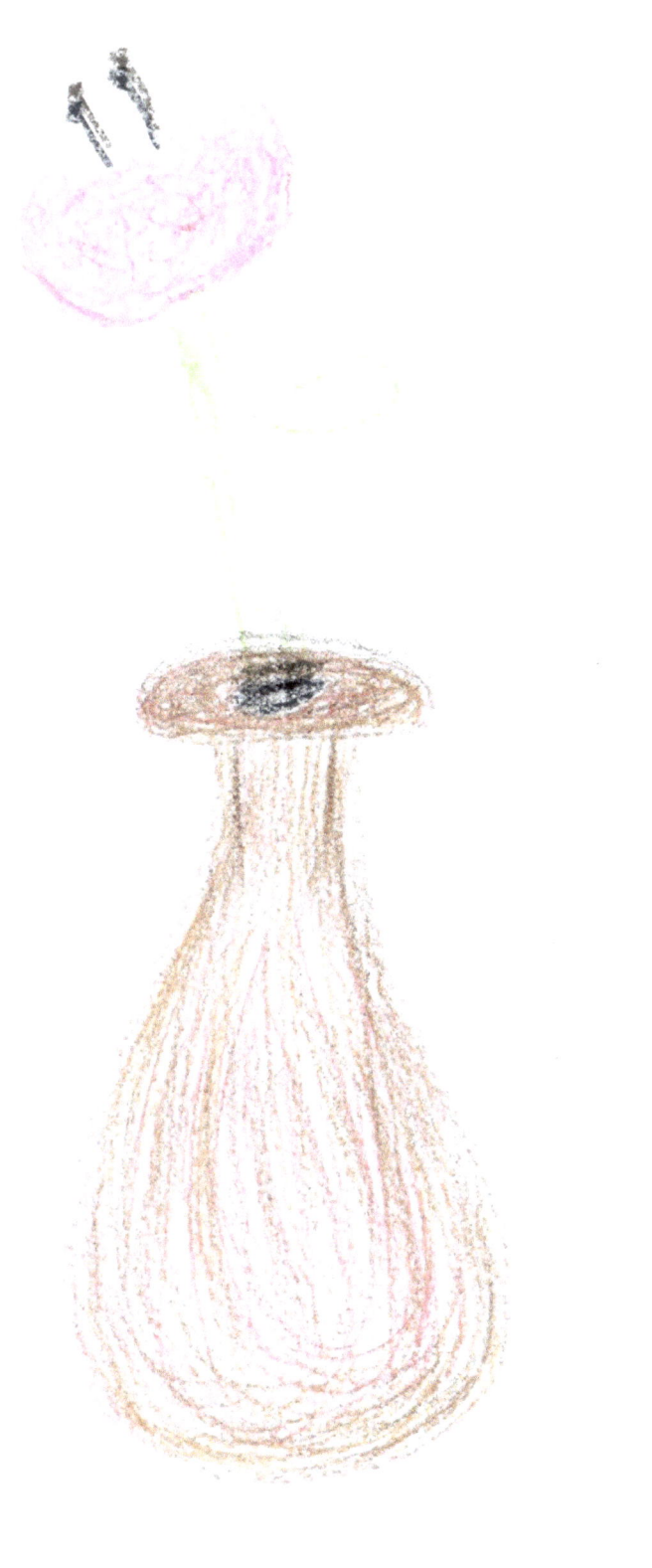

# Color Drawing 6

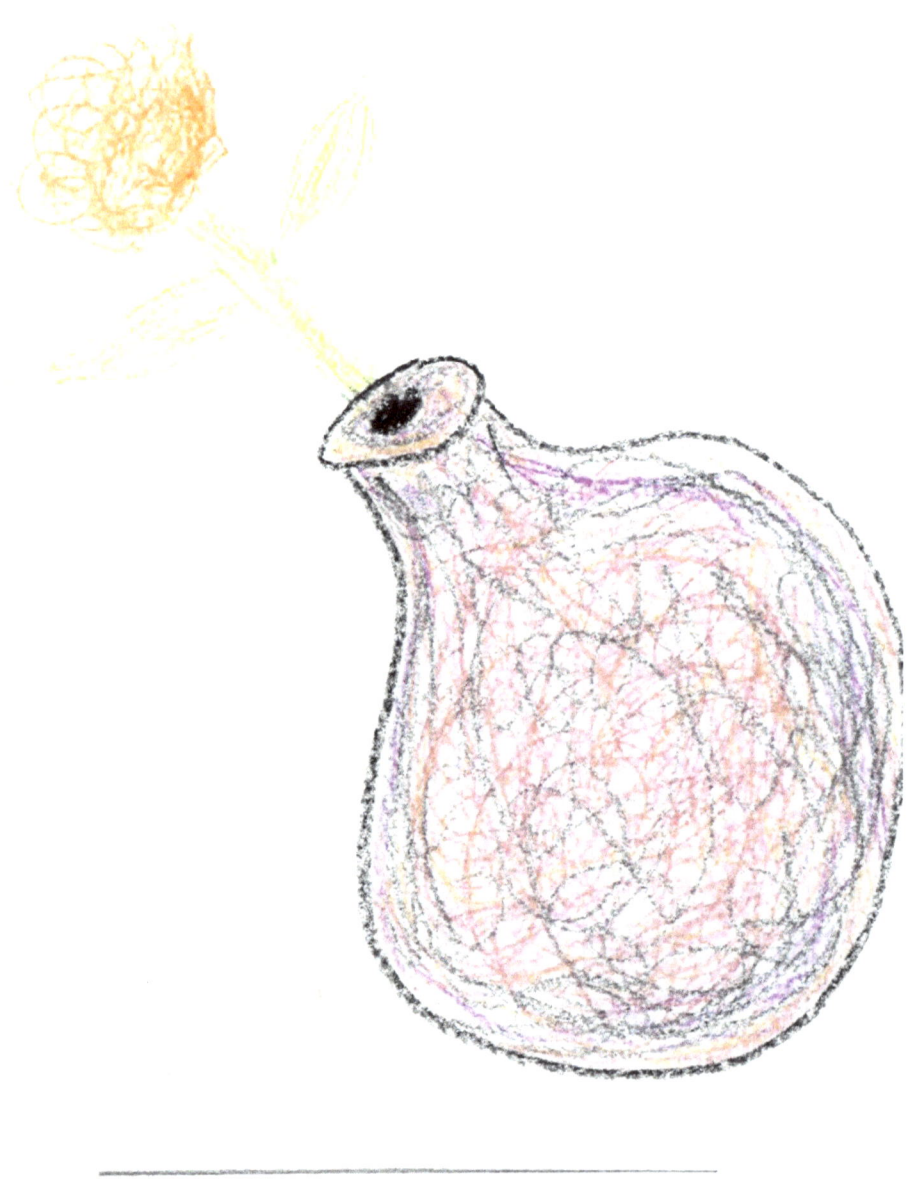

# Color Drawing 7

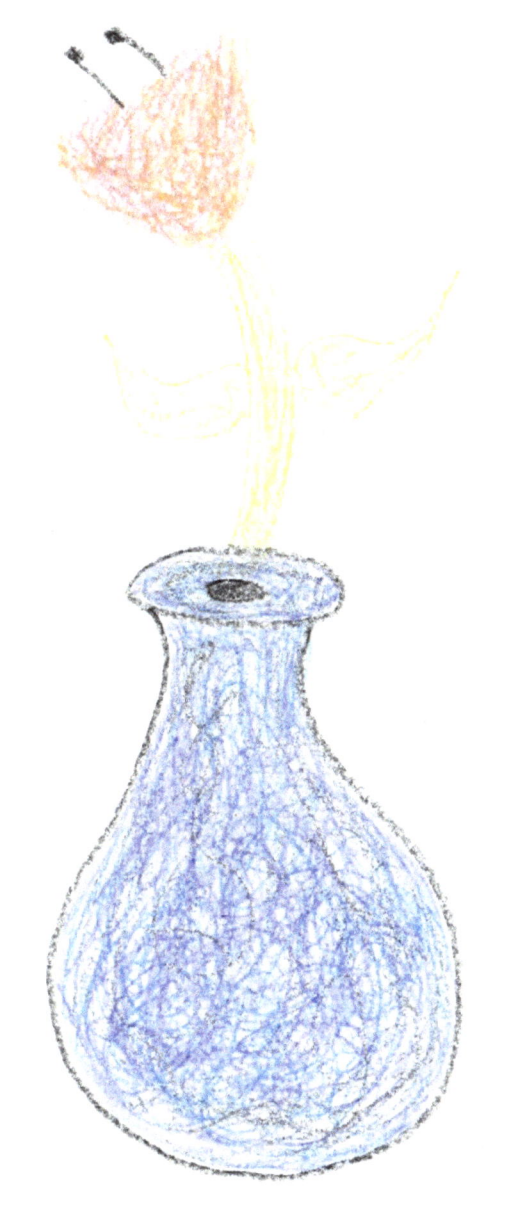

# Color Drawing 8

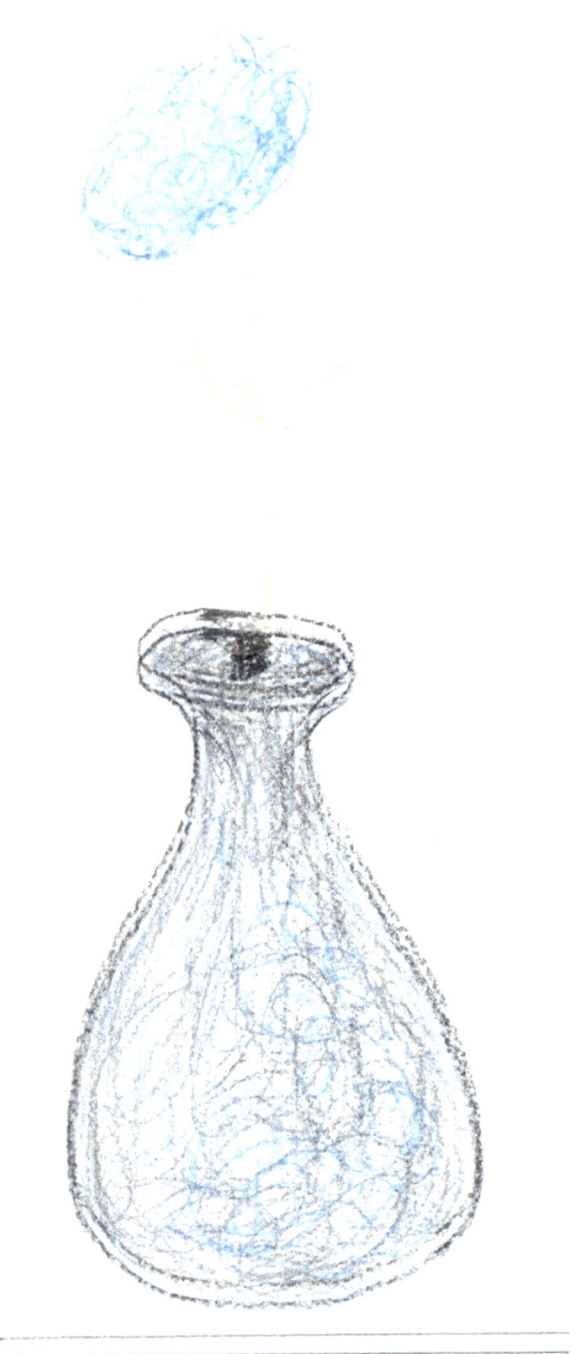

## Color Drawing 9

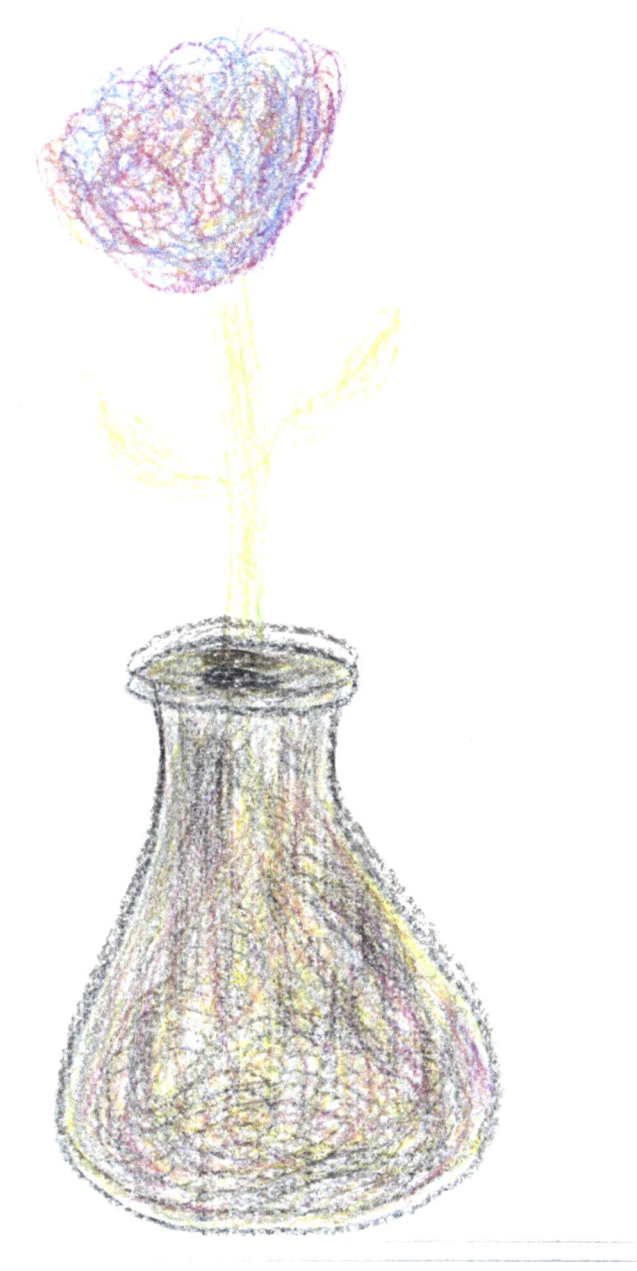

## Color Drawing 10

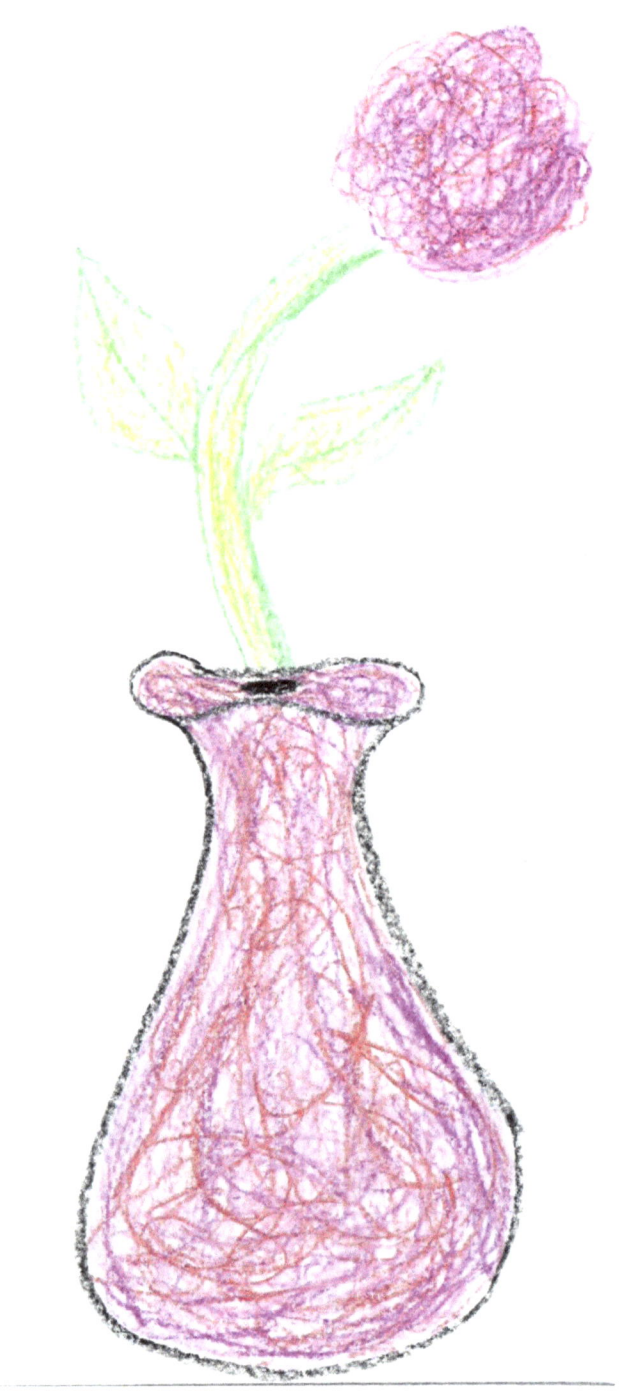

The End

Notes to Readers:

Cover:
See my first picture drawing where I drew a thick black horizontal line, drew seven small identical black circles equally spaced just beneath it, and colored each with a different crayon color.

Synopsis:
People respond to shapes and symbols. It is part of out human intelligence. Colors affect our emotions. It is apart of our sensitive feeling nature. Here is a collection of pencil drawings and crayon subjects to stimulate the reader's imagination. Some of these I have been drawing for many years. Instead of a book full of wordy text, I have escaped words to a degree into the realm of original creative art. As I enjoyed doing this book, I hope the readers find it to their liking.

Biography:
As a child I made drawings. I used crayons, pencils, and water colors to create images. Teachers in school taught me symbols, systems of knowledge, useful things, and cultural material. Here as a mature man I have returned to drawing again. The creative spark is behind it all.

www.ingramcontent.com/pod-product-compliance
Lightning Source LLC
Chambersburg PA
CBHW051937210526

45473CB00006B/2288